Too Hot?
Too Cold?

Keeping Body Temperature Just Right

Caroline Arnold

Illustrated by **Annie Patterson**

Charlesbridge

P9-DBV-803

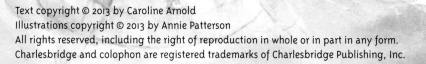

To my husband, Art—C. A.

For my friends on Alaska's North Slope, who truly know the meaning of cold, but whose hearts and homes are always warm—A. P.

Text copyright © 2013 by Caroline Arnold
Illustrations copyright © 2013 by Annie Patterson
All rights reserved, including the right of reproduction in whole or in part in any form.
Charlesbridge and colophon are registered trademarks of Charlesbridge Publishing, Inc.

Published by Charlesbridge
85 Main Street, Watertown, MA 02472
(617) 926-0329 • www.charlesbridge.com

Illustrations done in watercolor and Adobe Photoshop
Display type set in Chaloops by Chank and text type set in Triplex by Emigre
Color separations by KHL Chroma Graphics, Singapore
Printed and bound September 2012 by Imago in Singapore
Production supervision by Brian G. Walker
Designed by Whitney Leader-Picone

Library of Congress Cataloging-in-Publication Data
Arnold, Caroline.
   Too hot? too cold? : keeping body temperature just right / Caroline Arnold ;
Illustrated by Annie Patterson.
        p. cm.
     ISBN 978-1-58089-276-6 (reinforced for library use)
     ISBN 978-1-58089-277-3 (softcover)
1. Body temperature—Regulation—Juvenile literature. I. Patterson, Annie, 1975– ill.
II. Title.
QP135.A76 2013
612'.01426—dc23   2012000792

Printed in Singapore
(hc) 10 9 8 7 6 5 4 3 2 1
(sc) 10 9 8 7 6 5 4 3 2 1

Hot or Cold?

If you live in Alaska, you must put on warm clothes when you go outdoors on a cold winter day. If you live in Florida, you rarely need a jacket. Instead, you might take a swim or drink cold lemonade to help your body stay cool.

The temperature of the air around you varies from morning to night, from season to season, and from place to place. When it changes, processes within your body, such as shivering or sweating, can help you warm up or cool down. You can also change your behavior to adjust your temperature.

Animals are able to control their body temperature, too. They do it in many of the same ways you do.

Caribbean flamingos

Temperature Extremes. Living things do best when their bodies are within a certain temperature range. If an animal is too hot or too cold, its body processes do not work properly. Few animals can survive if their bodies are warmer than 114 degrees Fahrenheit. No animal can live if its body temperature falls below freezing.

Arctic fox

3

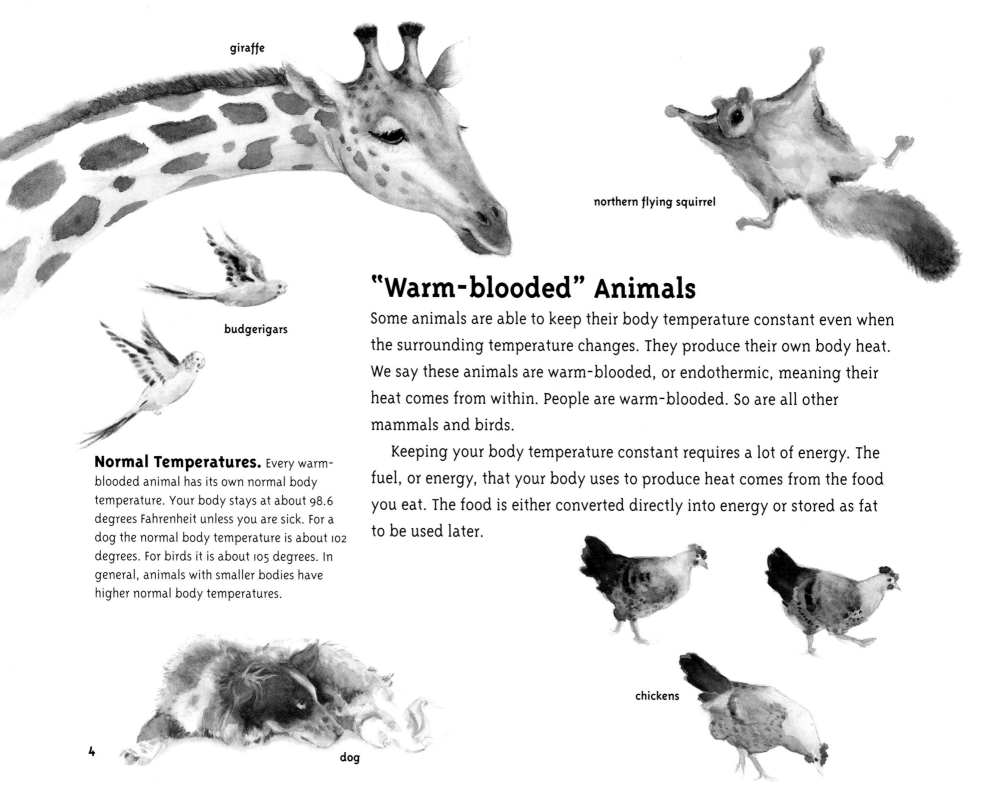

giraffe

northern flying squirrel

budgerigars

"Warm-blooded" Animals

Some animals are able to keep their body temperature constant even when the surrounding temperature changes. They produce their own body heat. We say these animals are warm-blooded, or endothermic, meaning their heat comes from within. People are warm-blooded. So are all other mammals and birds.

Keeping your body temperature constant requires a lot of energy. The fuel, or energy, that your body uses to produce heat comes from the food you eat. The food is either converted directly into energy or stored as fat to be used later.

Normal Temperatures. Every warm-blooded animal has its own normal body temperature. Your body stays at about 98.6 degrees Fahrenheit unless you are sick. For a dog the normal body temperature is about 102 degrees. For birds it is about 105 degrees. In general, animals with smaller bodies have higher normal body temperatures.

chickens

4

dog

Fever. When you are sick with an infection, your temperature may go up a few degrees. This is called a fever. Fever is the body's way of fighting the infection. Most germs that cause infections cannot live at higher than normal body temperatures.

Day and Night. Your body temperature varies slightly throughout the day. It is highest in the afternoon and lowest at night when you are sleeping.

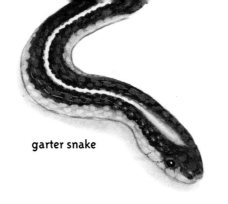
garter snake

green sea turtle

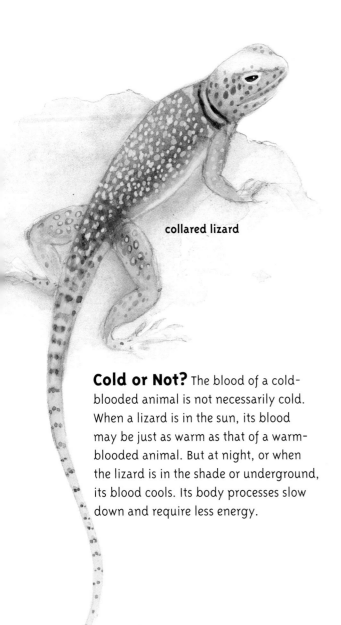
collared lizard

Cold or Not? The blood of a cold-blooded animal is not necessarily cold. When a lizard is in the sun, its blood may be just as warm as that of a warm-blooded animal. But at night, or when the lizard is in the shade or underground, its blood cools. Its body processes slow down and require less energy.

"Cold-blooded" Animals

Some animals have body temperatures that vary with their surroundings. They depend on getting heat from outside their bodies. We say they are cold-blooded, or ectothermic. Reptiles, amphibians, and fish are cold-blooded animals.

An ectothermic animal moves within its environment to adjust its body temperature. After a cool night an animal such as a lizard needs to warm up before becoming active. It may sunbathe or sit on a rock that has been warmed by the sun. When the lizard is warm enough, it goes in the shade.

rainbow trout

spotted salamander

Pacific tree frog

6

monarch butterfly

Insects. Insects and other invertebrates also have body temperatures that vary with their surroundings. Many insects cannot fly at temperatures much below one hundred degrees Fahrenheit. A butterfly warms up by sitting in the sun and opening its wings. Fluids in the wings are heated and then pumped into the body. If the butterfly becomes too hot, it turns its wings away from the sun.

Our Bodies Keep Us Warm or Cool

Your brain regulates your body heat. You have nerves in your skin that send messages to your brain. If your skin is hotter than the inside of your body, your brain tells your body to cool down. If your skin is cooler than your body, your brain tells your body to warm up. Processes within your body automatically adjust your temperature.

Moving Muscles

When your muscles contract to make you move, they produce heat. That is why you feel warm when you exercise. Muscles also produce heat by shivering. When you get chilled your brain tells your muscles to make small, rapid movements. This warms up your body without using a lot of extra energy.

Animals shiver, too. Mammals and birds shiver on chilly days to keep warm.

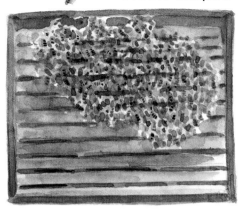

clustered honeybees

Heating the Hive. In winter honeybees cluster together inside their hive and warm up the air by vibrating their large wing muscles. They keep the hive at about 93.2 degrees Fahrenheit even when the temperature outside is below freezing.

ball python

Warm Eggs. Even snakes sometimes shiver. A female python curls around her eggs and vibrates her muscles. She can produce enough heat to keep the eggs as much as thirteen degrees Fahrenheit warmer than the surrounding air.

Sweating

When your body heats up from exercise, you may sweat. Sweating, or perspiring, is another way that your body controls its temperature. Sweat is mostly water with a little bit of salt. It is produced in your sweat glands and comes out of tiny holes in your skin called pores. As the sweat dries, it takes heat away from your body, and your skin feels cool.

Horses and humans are among the few animals that sweat to cool off. Most animals do not sweat very much—or at all.

surface of skin

sweat

pore

hair follicle

sweat gland

blood vessel

Sweat Glands. Did you know that you have 2.6 million sweat glands in your skin? People who live in hot climates can produce up to three quarts of sweat an hour!

Australian pelican

Panting. Dogs produce sweat only on their feet. Instead of sweating, a dog cools off by panting. As the dog breathes in air, its mouth, tongue, and lungs are cooled by evaporating moisture. Birds such as pelicans cool off in a similar way by flapping thin membranes in their throats to increase evaporation.

fennec fox

Escaping Heat. The fennec fox lives in the Sahara desert. As blood flows through its large ears, the fox's body heat escapes into the air.

Cooling and Warming the Blood

Does your face feel hot when you exercise on a warm day? The blood is rushing to the surface of your skin. When you are hot your brain tells the blood vessels in your skin to get bigger. Then the blood can cool off quickly because it is closer to the cooler outside air. When you are cold the blood vessels in your skin get smaller. Then it is harder for heat to escape, and more of your body heat stays inside. Animals retain and lose heat through their blood vessels, too.

walruses

Arctic cod

Shrinking Blood Vessels. Walruses live in the Arctic, where the water is icy cold. When a walrus is in the water, its blood vessels become so small that its skin looks almost white. When the walrus comes out of the water into the warmer air, the blood rushes back to its skin and it turns pink.

Natural Antifreeze. Surprisingly, some fish are able to live in near-freezing water. They have special proteins in their blood that act like antifreeze to keep ice crystals from forming.

13

snow buntings

Fur, Hair, and Feathers

Most warm-blooded animals are covered with fur or feathers. The hairs or feathers trap tiny pockets of warm air next to the body. You have hair on your head. It helps keep your head warm.

Feathers. An outer layer of long, smooth feathers protects a bird's body. An inner layer of soft down feathers traps heat and keeps the bird warm. Penguins have more than seventy feathers per square inch of skin. If a penguin is too warm, it may fluff up its feathers, as if opening a set of blinds, to let the air cool off its body.

rockhopper penguin

beaver

Fur. A beaver has two layers of fur. An inner layer of dense fur keeps it warm. Longer outer hairs help keep the beaver dry.

hair

skin

goose bump

Goose Bumps. When you get chilled, tiny muscles in your skin tighten and make the hairs on your arms and legs stand up. Because the hair on your arms and legs is thin, you can see the tiny lumps the muscles make under the skin. These are called goose bumps.

15

Fat

You have a layer of fat under your skin. It is like a built-in blanket that helps protect your body and keep it warm. Fat is a good insulator. It holds in your body heat. Some animals, such as bears, put on extra fat before winter. The fat helps keep them warm when the weather is cold and provides energy when food is scarce.

polar bears

Brown Fat. Most fat is white, but smaller amounts of brown fat are also found in the body, especially in young animals and animals that hibernate. Brown fat has the unique ability to produce heat. It helps keep newborn animals warm before they develop a cushion of white fat to insulate their small bodies.

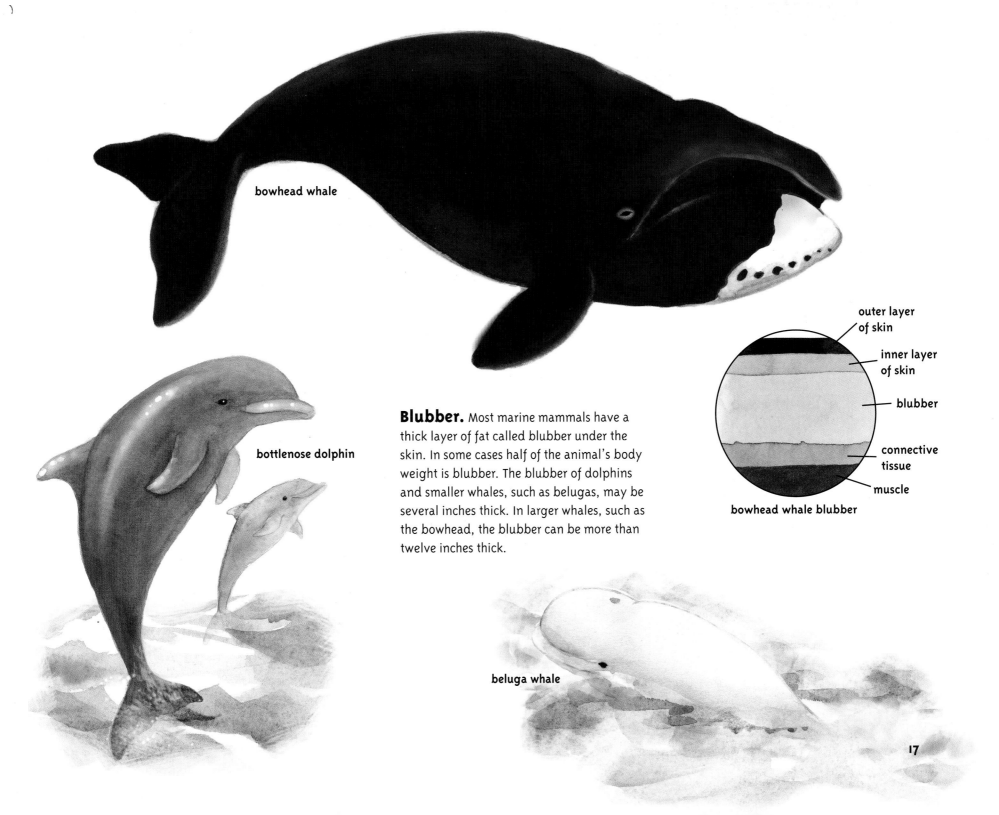

bowhead whale

bottlenose dolphin

Blubber. Most marine mammals have a thick layer of fat called blubber under the skin. In some cases half of the animal's body weight is blubber. The blubber of dolphins and smaller whales, such as belugas, may be several inches thick. In larger whales, such as the bowhead, the blubber can be more than twelve inches thick.

outer layer of skin

inner layer of skin

blubber

connective tissue

muscle

bowhead whale blubber

beluga whale

American crocodile

Big Bodies. A crocodile's huge body helps it retain body heat longer than a smaller reptile could. This lets it remain active even after the sun has gone down.

Body Size and Shape

An animal's body shape affects its ability to stay warm. For example, on a hot day a cat stretches out its body and lies in the shade. On a cold day the cat curls up in a ball. A compact shape has less surface area exposed to the air, so the cat stays warmer when it is curled up and cooler when it is stretched out.

Animals with large bodies warm up and cool down more slowly than smaller animals. They have less surface area in relation to their size than smaller animals do.

cougar

Sharing Warmth. Keeping close together helps animals stay warm. Emperor penguins huddle together in groups of up to six thousand birds during fierce Antarctic snowstorms. In the group an individual penguin loses heat only half as fast as it would alone.

emperor penguins

lappet-faced vulture

What We Do to Be Warm or Cool

Your behavior is another way you adjust your body temperature so that you are comfortable.

Sunbathing

The sun is like a furnace in the sky. It warms the Earth. It feels good to go out in the sun on a cool morning. Many animals like to sit in the sun to warm up, too. Dark colors are good for absorbing the sun's heat. On cold mornings vultures hold up their wide, dark wings and face the sun.

Reflecting the Sun. Light colors reflect the sun and help keep an animal cool. The addax, an antelope that lives on the Arabian Peninsula, has a light-colored summer coat to help protect it from the hot desert sun.

Safe in the Sun. The sun's rays provide warmth. But they can also damage your skin. That's why we put on sunscreen and wear hats when spending time outdoors.

addaxes

20

Finding a Cool Breeze

One way you can cool off on a warm day is by sitting in front of a fan. As cooler, moving air passes your body, it takes away heat. Animals also like to find cool breezes on a warm day. Birds may perch at the top of a tree or on a windy cliff by the edge of the sea.

Japanese white-eye

Out of the Wind. In winter the wind makes the air feel even colder than the actual temperature. We call this the wind-chill factor. Then birds may perch under a ledge or find another protected place to stay warm.

tufted duck

A Cool Swim

Water can help you cool off on a hot day. You can take a cold shower, play in a sprinkler, or swim. The cool water on your skin helps lower your body temperature. Your body also cools off as it dries after you come out of the water.

Animals like to cool off in water, too. Water cools off the body much faster than air. A warm-blooded animal loses heat twenty-five times faster in the water than in air of the same temperature.

Shower Bath. Have you ever seen an elephant give itself a shower? As it squirts water over its back, its large body loses heat.

African elephant

Hawaiian monk seal

Wet Sand. Some animals keep cool by lying in mud or wet sand. On warm days in Hawaii, monk seals sometimes come onshore to rest in wet sand.

A Hot Bath

Water can also help you get warm. When you are chilled, a hot bath warms you up. In some parts of the world, natural hot springs are hot baths for animals.

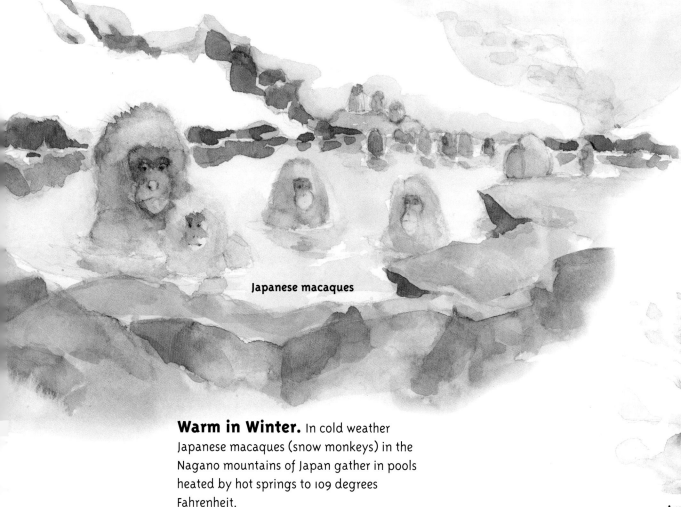

Japanese macaques

Warm in Winter. In cold weather Japanese macaques (snow monkeys) in the Nagano mountains of Japan gather in pools heated by hot springs to 109 degrees Fahrenheit.

Hot Steam. In Yellowstone National Park, in Wyoming, hot steam puffs out of the earth. Bison gather around these steam vents in winter to get warm.

American bison

23

kangaroo rat

Nocturnal Life. In hot climates, one way to avoid the heat is to stay inside during the day and go out at night when the air is cooler. The kangaroo rat, a small rodent that lives in the deserts of the western United States, comes out of its burrow only at night to hunt for seeds.

Out of the Weather

When it is too cold or too hot to stay outside, you go indoors. Many animals also seek shelter to avoid extreme temperatures. They may go inside a hollow tree, into a cave, or underground.

Cold-blooded animals such as fish, frogs, snakes, and turtles have no internal way to keep warm during the winter. Instead, they find shelter in places that stay above freezing. Many reptiles go into holes or burrows. Fish may float at the bottom of a pond. A frog may find a damp place under leaves or mud. The animals cool down and spend the winter inactive, or dormant. When spring comes their bodies warm up and they become active again.

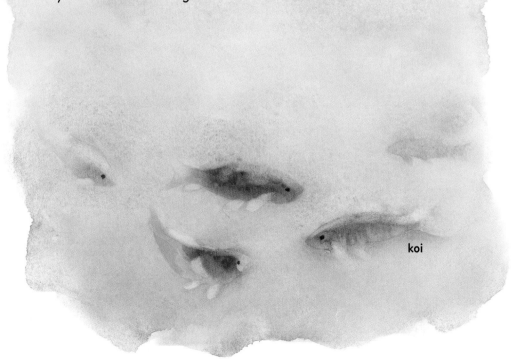

koi

A Cozy Burrow. Wombats are ground-dwelling marsupials that live in Australia. Their underground burrows stay cool and humid even on the hottest summer days; in winter the temperature of the burrow rarely falls below forty degrees Fahrenheit. Whatever the weather, the wombats can be comfortable underground.

wombats

little brown bats

Hibernating

Some warm-blooded animals deal with cold weather by hibernating through the winter. Their breathing and heart rate slow, and their temperature drops. Body fat is converted to energy. Because the animals are inactive, they can survive on very little energy. They may remain inactive for just a few days or up to several months.

A Long Hibernation. Many bats hibernate through the winter in caves or hollow trees. A little brown bat may hibernate for up to eighty-three days. Its body temperature drops almost to freezing, it breathes only once a minute, and its heart rate slows from four hundred to twenty-five beats a minute.

Torpor. Even during the summer a bat's body temperature varies. During the day, when the bat is inactive, its body temperature drops several degrees. This is called daily torpor. Torpor helps the bat save energy for flying at night.

Estivating. Sometimes animals that live in very hot climates slow down their bodies in the summer or during dry periods. This kind of inactivity is called estivation and is similar to hibernation. Lungfish, which live in Africa and South America, estivate by burrowing into mud and becoming dormant when rivers and water holes dry up.

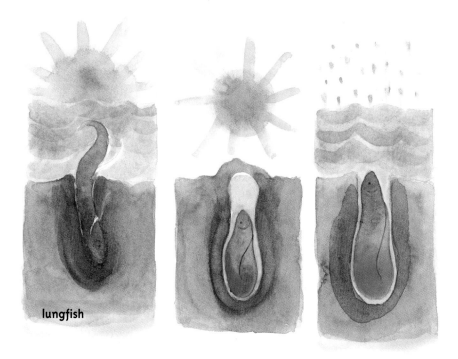

lungfish

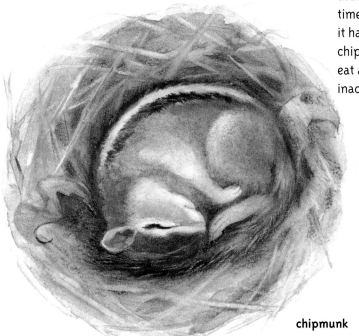

chipmunk

A Short Hibernation. A chipmunk usually hibernates for just a few days at a time, waking up periodically to eat food that it has stored in its underground den. The chipmunk's body warms when it wakes up to eat and then cools when it goes back to its inactive state.

A Hibernating Bird. Most birds do not hibernate. One exception is the common poorwill, a nocturnal bird found in western North America. Hidden among rocks, the common poorwill may remain inactive for weeks or months at a time.

common poorwill

ruby-throated
hummingbird

greater white-fronted geese

Migrating

Some animals leave their homes, or migrate, when the weather gets too cold or too hot. In the northern hemisphere some animals go south for the winter and north for the summer. In the southern hemisphere they move north in winter and south in summer. Many birds migrate. So do some fish, turtles, butterflies, and mammals like reindeer and caribou. Animals migrate to find food, safe places for their young, and a more comfortable climate.

Winter in Mexico. Ruby-throated hummingbirds spend the summer in the United States and Canada sipping nectar from summer flowers. In fall, as the weather turns cool and plants stop flowering, the hummingbirds fly south to Mexico for the winter.

humpback whales

Winter in Hawaii. Pacific humpback whales spend the summer in the oceans of Alaska, but when winter comes and the oceans begin to freeze, they swim to the warm waters of Hawaii.

Too Hot? Too Cold? Just Right.

You feel best when you are not too hot and not too cold. Your body helps keep you at the right temperature. Your behavior helps you to adjust your temperature, too.

People and animals live in hot places and cold places all over the world. Whether you live in the icy Arctic like a polar bear, a steamy tropical rainforest like a tree frog, or the vast Sahara desert like a fennec fox, you can stay warm or cool. In every climate, people and animals find ways to keep their body temperature just right.

mallard ducks

Glossary

amphibian—a cold-blooded vertebrate that spends part of its life on land and part in water

blubber—the thick layer of fat between the skin and muscle layers of whales and other marine mammals

cold-blooded—another word for ectothermic

dormant—inactive

ectothermic—having a body temperature determined by the environment

endothermic—producing heat within the body

estivate—to pass the summer or dry season in an inactive state

hibernate—to pass the winter in an inactive state

invertebrate—an animal without a backbone

mammal—a warm-blooded animal that gives birth to live young and feeds its babies milk

marsupial—a mammal that carries its young in a pouch

membrane—a thin layer of skin or tissue

migrate—to move to another location with the seasons

perspire—to sweat

protein—one of the substances necessary to build and maintain plant and animal cells

reptile—a cold-blooded, scaly vertebrate, such as a snake or lizard, that creeps or crawls

rodent—a gnawing mammal

torpor—a short-term drop in body temperature, heart rate, breathing, and other body functions

vertebrate—an animal with a backbone

warm-blooded—another word for endothermic

Author's Note

In this book I have used the common terms "warm-blooded" and "cold-blooded" to make the general principles of temperature regulation easier to understand and remember. The terms are a simplification. Scientists prefer to use "endothermic" and "ectothermic" to distinguish between animals that produce their own body heat and those that don't. They use "homeothermic" and "poikilothermic" to distinguish between animals that maintain a constant body temperature and those that don't. Most endotherms are homeotherms and most ectotherms are poikilotherms, but there are many exceptions to the rule.

NORTHVILLE DISTRICT LIBRARY

3 9082 12250 6747